Pet Perspectives

Contents

Should People Keep Rats as Pets?

Predict...

What do you think the arguments for and against keeping rats as pets might be?

intelligent

Opinion One

People should be allowed to keep rats as pets.

Today, there are many types of rats that have been specially bred to be pets. Specially bred rats are easy to care for and keep clean, and they are companionable and amusing. Rats are companionable because they are intelligent and friendly animals. They are capable of various antics and can even be trained to perform tricks. Rats are amusing because they are more fun to watch than cats or goldfish. They also have interesting physical characteristics, such as bright beady eyes, long twitching whiskers and elongated tails.

Finally, pet rats require only minimal care because they keep themselves clean, unlike dogs! Dogs need regular shampooing, and as for goldfish their owners have to clean out aquariums filled with decaying food and slime!

In my opinion, people should be allowed to keep rats because they make desirable pets.

companionable

Clarify!

antics

A   mischief
B   jokes
C   stunts
A, B or C?

amusing

Inference

What inferences can you make about the character of a person who would support Opinion Two?

People should not be allowed to keep rats as pets.

Rats can be destructive pests, they can carry diseases and they are smelly. Throughout history, people have attempted to eradicate rats because they are pests. Rats use their long front teeth to gnaw anything and everything. If kept in a house, a pet rat could destroy lots of things, such as books and clothes. Scientific research has shown that rats carry microscopic germs that may spread to other animals. People would be irresponsible to keep a rat as a pet knowing that they may spread germs. Finally, rats smell disgusting! Keeping a rat in a house might make it smell offensive.

In my opinion, people should not be allowed to keep rats as pets.

destructive

After considering both sides of the argument, I believe that people should be allowed to keep rats as pets. Rats are companionable and easy to look after. Any animal can be destructive if its owner allows it to be. Also any animal will carry disease if it is not properly cared for. People should not be prejudiced against pet rats because of their experiences with rats in the wild.

should not be prejudiced

Clarify!

prejudiced

A biased

B fair

C neutral

A, B or C?

Summary

Opinion 1

People **should** be allowed to keep rats as pets.

What are the main arguments to support this opinion?

Opinion 2

People **should not** be allowed to keep rats as pets.

What are the main arguments to support this opinion?

Should Pets Be Returnable?

Predict...

What do you think the arguments for and against pets being returnable might be?

one-month trial

Opinion One

People should be able to return pets after one month.

Many people don't realise how difficult and costly it is to look after a pet until it is too late. Sometimes, people abandon their pet when it becomes annoying or too much work. This is cruel. Pets are usually domesticated and not equipped to fend for themselves. Abandoned pets may become malnourished, as they are unable to find food for themselves. Animal shelters are overflowing with abandoned animals, many of which have to be put down.

A one-month trial period would give people time to adjust. It would provide new owners with the time to investigate whether their chosen pet suits their lifestyle. If the pet is too much of an inconvenience, or is too troublesome, it could be returned to the pet shop instead of being abandoned or neglected. This is a more humane and sensible approach and would result in fewer pets being abandoned.

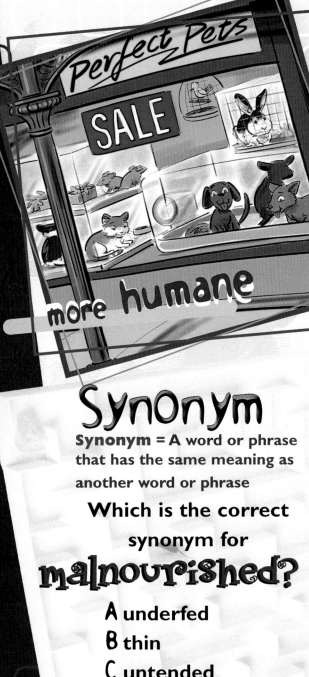

more humane

sensible

Synonym

Synonym = A word or phrase that has the same meaning as another word or phrase

Which is the correct synonym for malnourished?

A underfed
B thin
C untended

A, B or C?

Antonym

Antonym = A word or phrase that is opposite in meaning to another word or phrase

Which is the correct antonym for

abandoned?

A well behaved
B kept
C chosen

A, B or C?

Question?

Why do you think people would need to ensure their home was a suitable environment for a pet?

Opinion Two

Pets should not be returnable.

Pets are living, breathing animals, not returnable goods. They deserve a stable, loving environment with people who are committed to looking after them. People need to consider their ability to care for a pet before they buy one. They need to research the costs involved, the animal's needs and their own ability to address these needs. They must ensure their home is a suitable environment for the pet and that all family members are willing to accept the added responsibility.

If pets could be returned after one month, people might buy a pet on impulse, only to return the animal when they tire of it or realise it was a poor choice. How confused would the animal feel to find itself back in the pet shop each month? Animals have feelings and would suffer if they were continually returned to the pet shop. Imagine how hurt and upset you would be if your parents returned you!

Pets are not returnable goods!

11

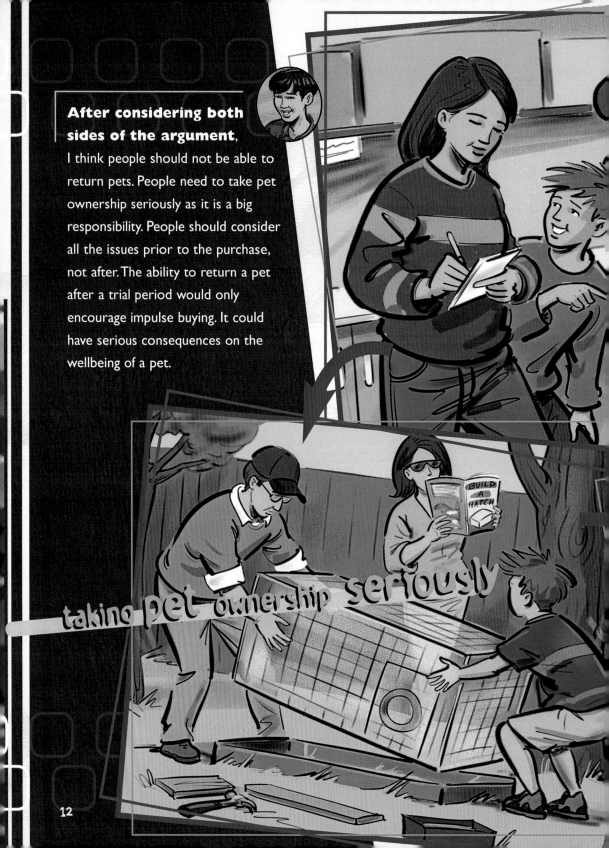

After considering both sides of the argument, I think people should not be able to return pets. People need to take pet ownership seriously as it is a big responsibility. People should consider all the issues prior to the purchase, not after. The ability to return a pet after a trial period would only encourage impulse buying. It could have serious consequences on the wellbeing of a pet.

taking pet ownership seriously

Summary

Opinion 1

Pets **should** be returnable.

What are the main arguments to support this opinion?

Opinion 2

Pets **should not** be returnable.

What are the main arguments to support this opinion?

Does Every Family Need a Pet?

Predict...

What do you think the arguments for and against every family needing a pet might be?

learn to care for another

Opinion One

Every family needs a pet.

Research supports the belief that people who keep pets develop desirable characteristics. This is because many pets are totally dependent on their owners for food and shelter. When a family has to meet the needs of a dependant, its members are provided with the opportunity to be responsible. What a great way for children to learn responsibility – more effective than performing chores like putting out the rubbish!

Pet ownership provides family members with the chance to nurture another being. Often, this results in individuals developing a more compassionate attitude towards others. Pets also provide companionship. If every family had a pet, there would be less loneliness.

I think the world would be a better place if all families had to care for a pet. The community would benefit if future generations were reliable, responsible and caring.

learning responsibility

Clarify!
generations

A people
B age groups
C children

A, B or C?

Inference

What inferences can be made about the ways in which pets provide companionship?

Question?

What do you think is the best argument against every family needing a pet? Why?

costly equipment

Opinion Two

Not every family needs or wants a pet.

Firstly, pets are expensive. They cost money to purchase and they are costly to keep. They require balanced diets and regular visits to the vet. They often require expensive equipment, such as cages, tanks, rugs and grooming tools. Not every family can afford to look after a pet, and some families have other ways they wish to spend their money.

Secondly, a pet is a big responsibility. Each pet has needs that can only be met by its owners. Most pets need washing, grooming and exercise. Some families are too busy to look after a pet properly, which may result in the pets being neglected.

Only families that want a pet should have one. Think of those pets that live with people who do not like animals or do not have the time, money or desire to look after a pet properly. Imagine how miserable their lives might be.

After considering both sides of the argument, I think that while there are many benefits in caring for a pet, not every family should have one. People should have the right to choose whether or not to have a pet. People should not be forced to take on the responsibility and expense of having a pet if they do not want one. And it is not fair for an animal to live with someone who does not want or cannot afford a pet.

the right to choose

Fact or Opinion?

Fact = A statement that can be proved to be true

Opinion = A view or belief that is not based on fact or knowledge

Fact	opinion
Most pets need washing, grooming and exercise.	People should have the right to choose whether or not to have a pet.

Go back through the debates to find more examples of facts and opinion.

BIRD SEED

FOOD

WATER

Think About the Text

Making connections – What connections can you make to the text?

Thinking logically

Identifying with viewpoints

Getting your message across

Text to Self

Being forceful

Thinking quickly

Formulating opinions

Being persuasive

Supporting opinion with evidence

Text to Text

Talk about other debate texts you have read that have similar features to the debates in *Pet Perspectives*. Compare the texts.

Text to World

Talk about situations in the world that might connect to elements in the text.

Planning a Written Debate

1 Decide on an issue
Some people believe rats make good pets.

2 Present arguments to support the statement

Rats are easy to care for and to keep clean.

Rats are companionable.

Rats are amusing.

3 Present arguments against the statement

Rats are destructive.

Rats can carry diseases.

Rats are smelly.

4 Decide on which viewpoints you agree with

yes

People should not be prejudiced against rats.

Rats are good companions.

Rats specially bred to be pets do not carry diseases.

5 Write your conclusion
After considering both sides of the argument, I believe that people should be allowed to keep rats as pets.

Written Debates
should feature

- An opening statement that presents the issues.

- Opposing and supporting opinions with logical examples to support these opinions.

- Short paragraphs and sentences.

- Phrases such as 'I think ...', 'we believe ...', 'in my opinion ...'

- A knowledge of the subject.

- A final statement in which the author's stand on the issue is made after both sides of the issue have been considered.

VET BILL $1,000